Affluence without money

AFFLUENCE WITHOUT FINANCES

Boost Your Property Acquisition with Subject-to, Seller Finance, and Other Innovative Solutions

By

FERRAN JESSE

Affluence without money

Table of contents

Acknowledgement

Introduction

Chapter one
Mindset and Attitude
- Developing a positive mindset and attitude towards money and material possessions
- Learning to appreciate what you have

Chapter two
Relationships
- Cultivating meaningful relationships and social connections
- Sharing resources and skills with others

Chapter three
Health and Well-being
- Prioritizing self-care and wellness

Chapter four
Creativity and Resourcefulness
- Using creativity and resourcefulness to solve problems

- Finding alternative ways to acquire goods and services

Chapter five
Community Involvement
- Getting involved in local community initiatives
- Building a sense of community and belongings

Conclusion

ACKNOWLEDGEMENT

Acknowledging affluence without finances is important because it recognizes the value and importance of non-material aspects of life and the benefits that can come from focusing on these areas. It is an acknowledgment of the fact that wealth and material possessions are not the only things that bring happiness, fulfillment, and abundance to our lives.

Acknowledging affluence without finances can take many forms, such as expressing gratitude for the simple pleasures in life, celebrating accomplishments that have nothing to do with financial success, recognizing the value of human connections and experiences, and promoting a culture that values personal growth and well-being over material wealth.

By acknowledging and embracing affluence without finances, we can shift our focus away from the constant pursuit of material possessions and instead cultivate a deeper appreciation for the intangible things that bring joy and meaning to our lives. This can lead to greater happiness, reduced stress, stronger relationships, and a more fulfilling and meaningful existence.

INTRODUCTION

Affluence without **finances** refers to a lifestyle where a person feels wealthy, abundant, and fulfilled without relying on material possessions or wealth. It's about finding contentment and happiness in experiences, relationships, and personal growth rather than accumulating material goods.

This lifestyle emphasizes the importance of living simply, embracing minimalism, and focusing on what truly matters in life. It often involves practices such as mindfulness, gratitude, and conscious consumerism.

People who live an affluent lifestyle without **finances** may prioritize experiences over possessions, such as spending time in nature, engaging in creative activities, or pursuing personal interests. They may also value connections with others and prioritize building meaningful relationships over accumulating wealth or status.

Living an affluent lifestyle without **finances** can lead to a greater sense of freedom and inner peace, as well as reduced stress and anxiety related to financial pressures. It's a mindset that can benefit anyone, regardless of their financial situation, and can ultimately lead to a more fulfilling and satisfying life.

WHY PURSUING AFFLUENCE WITHOUT **FINANCES** IS IMPORTANT

Pursuing affluence without **finances** is important for several reasons:

1. **Reducing financial stress:** Living an affluence without **finances** lifestyle can help reduce financial stress and anxiety by emphasizing the importance of living within one's means, avoiding debt, and focusing on non-material sources of happiness and fulfillment.

Environmental sustainability: By prioritizing experiences over possessions and practicing conscious consumerism, individuals who pursue affluence without **finances** can help reduce their environmental footprint and contribute to a more sustainable world.

Greater freedom and flexibility: By not being tied down by material possessions, individuals who pursue affluence without money may experience greater freedom and flexibility in their lives. They may have more time and resources to pursue their passions, travel, and spend time with loved ones.

Improved well-being: By focusing on experiences, relationships, personal growth, and inner peace, individuals who pursue affluence without **finances** can experience greater well-being, happiness, and satisfaction in life. They may also develop a greater sense of purpose and fulfillment.

Overall, pursuing affluence without **finances** can lead to a more fulfilling, sustainable, and balanced way of life that emphasizes personal growth, meaningful experiences, and healthy relationships rather than material wealth and possessions.

CHAPTER ONE
MINDSET AND ATTITUDE

Developing a positive mindset and attitude towards money and material possessions can have a significant impact on your overall well-being and financial success. Here are some tips to help you cultivate a positive mindset towards money and material possessions:

1. **Recognize the value of money:** Money is a tool that can be used to create opportunities, fulfill needs, and make a difference in the world. By recognizing its value, you can develop a healthy relationship with money and understand how to use it effectively.

2. **Focus on abundance:** Instead of focusing on what you don't have, focus on what you do have. Cultivate an attitude of gratitude for what you have and believe that more good things are on the way. This mindset can help attract more abundance into your life.

3. **Avoid comparison**: It's easy to compare yourself to others and feel like you don't measure up. But the truth is, everyone's journey is different. Instead of comparing yourself to others, concentrate on your own goals and aspirations. Celebrate your progress and achievements, no matter how small they may feel.

4. **Create a budget:** A budget can help you gain control of your finances and reduce stress. By creating a budget, you can allocate your money towards the things that matter most to you, such as paying off debt or saving for a vacation.

5. **Learn about personal finance:** The more you know about personal finance, the more confident you will feel about your financial decisions. Take the time to educate yourself about investing, saving, and budgeting. This knowledge can help you make informed decisions that can benefit you in the long run.

6. **Give back:** Giving back to others can help you develop a positive relationship with money and material possessions. When you give to others, you experience the joy of helping others, which can help shift your focus away from material possessions and towards a more fulfilling life.

Remember, developing a positive mindset towards money and material possessions takes time and effort. But by following these tips, you can begin to shift your perspective and create a more positive relationship with money.

LEARNING TO APPRECIATE WHAT YOU DON'T HAVE

This means recognizing and valuing the good things in your life rather than focusing on what you don't have or what you wish you had. It involves shifting your mindset from one of lack to one of abundance and gratitude. There are several benefits to learning to appreciate what you have.

Firstly, it can help you feel happier and more content with your life as you begin to focus on what is good rather than what is lacking. It can also help you feel more connected to the people around you as you begin to appreciate their contributions to your life.

Additionally, it can help you cultivate a sense of resilience and perspective. When you encounter challenges or setbacks, being grateful for what you have can help you see the situation in a more positive light and find the strength to persevere.

There are many different ways to practice gratitude and learn to appreciate what you have.

Some people find it helpful to keep a gratefulness journal, where they write down effects, they are thankful for each day. Others practice mindfulness, which involves focusing on the present moment and becoming more aware of your thoughts and emotions. Engaging in acts of kindness and generosity towards others can also help you appreciate the good things in your life.

Affluence without money

Overall, it is a powerful tool for living a happier and more fulfilling life. It can help you cultivate a positive mindset and find joy in the present moment, regardless of the circumstances you find yourself in.

CHAPTER TWO
RELATIONSHIP
Cultivate meaningful relationships and social connections.

Cultivating a meaningful relationship refers to the intentional effort put into developing a deeper and more significant connection with someone that goes beyond surface-level interactions. This involves actively engaging with the other person and investing time and energy in building trust, mutual understanding, and emotional intimacy. Such relationships often involve sharing values, beliefs, and experiences and supporting each other in times of need.

Social connection, on the other hand, refers to the sense of belonging and interpersonal engagement that one experiences within a community or social network. This can take many forms, from close relationships with family and friends to more casual interactions with acquaintances and colleagues. Social connections are essential for our mental and emotional well-being and can help us feel supported, valued, and connected to something greater than ourselves.

Both cultivating meaningful relationships and social connections involve building and maintaining meaningful connections with others, but they differ in terms of the level of intimacy and the scope of the relationship. While cultivating meaningful relationships often involves a more intentional and focused effort on the part of the individuals involved, social connections can develop organically through shared experiences and interests within a larger social group.

Cultivating meaningful relationships and social connections is an essential aspect of human life, as it can significantly contribute to our happiness, well-being, and overall quality of life. Here are some tips on how to cultivate meaningful relationships and social connections:

- **Be intentional**: Cultivating meaningful relationships and social connections requires intentionality. This means making a deliberate effort to build and maintain relationships by investing time, energy, and resources.

- **Be open-minded:** Be open to meeting new people and forming new relationships. It is essential to be open to new experiences, ideas, and perspectives, as they can enrich your life.
- **Build trust:** Trust is essential in any relationship. Building trust takes time, but it is crucial to establish mutual respect, honesty, and reliability to form a strong and meaningful connection.
- **Communicate effectively:** Effective communication is key to maintaining healthy relationships. Listening actively, expressing yourself clearly, and practicing empathy and understanding can go a long way in creating meaningful connections
- **Prioritize quality over quantity:** It's not the number of relationships that matters, but the quality of those relationships. Concentrate on building deep, meaningful connections with people who share your values and interests.

- **Nurture existing relationships**: Maintain and nurture existing relationships by regularly connecting with friends and loved ones, checking in on them, and showing appreciation for their presence in your life.
- **Participate in community activities:** Participating in community activities and events can be an excellent way to meet new people and form connections. Joining clubs, volunteering, or attending social gatherings can provide opportunities to build meaningful relationships.

In conclusion, cultivating meaningful relationships and social connections is an ongoing process that requires intentionality, trust, effective communication, and a willingness to be open-minded. Prioritizing quality over quantity, nurturing existing relationships, and participating in community activities are all excellent ways to cultivate and maintain meaningful relationships.

SHARING RESOURCES AND SKILLS WITH OTHERS

This refers to the act of providing access to one's possessions, knowledge, abilities, or expertise to those who need or want them. It involves sharing physical or digital resources, such as tools, equipment, money, or information, as well as offering assistance, guidance, and mentoring.

It is often motivated by a desire to help, support, or empower others, as well as foster collaboration, community-building, and social cohesion. It can take many forms, such as donating money to a charity, lending a tool to a neighbor, teaching a skill to a friend, volunteering at a local organization, or participating in a collaborative project.

It can have numerous benefits, both for the giver and the receiver. It can help build trust, establish stronger social connections, increase mutual support and cooperation, and enhance individual and collective well-being.

Additionally, it can facilitate the transfer of knowledge and expertise, promote innovation and creativity, and contribute to the development of new ideas and solutions.

CHAPTER THREE
HEALTH AND WELL-BEING

Health and well-being are two related concepts that are fundamental to a person's quality of life. Health refers to the state of being physically and mentally fit, free from disease or injury, and having good functioning of all body systems. In other words, it's the absence of physical or mental illness.

On the other hand, well-being is a broader term that encompasses physical, mental, and emotional health, as well as social and spiritual aspects of life. It includes a sense of purpose and meaning in life, positive relationships, a sense of belonging, and the ability to cope with stress and challenges. Well-being is not just the absence of negative emotions; it's a positive state of being where an individual feels happy, content, and fulfilled.

Maintaining good health is essential for overall well-being, but it is not the only factor. Well-being also includes factors like having positive relationships, engaging in fulfilling work, practicing self-care, and feeling a sense of community and purpose. It's important to note that health and well-being are subjective and can vary from person to person. For some people, good health might be the most important aspect of their well-being, while for others, a sense of fulfillment or purpose might be more critical. Ultimately, health and well-being are closely linked, and both are essential for leading a fulfilling and happy life.

PRIORITIZING SELF-CARE AND WELLNESS

Prioritizing self-care and wellness means making a conscious decision to focus on your physical, mental, and emotional health. It involves taking care of yourself in a way that promotes overall well-being and helps you feel your best.

There are several different aspects of self-care and wellness that you can focus on. One important area is physical health, which includes things like getting regular exercise, eating a healthy diet, and getting enough sleep. When you take care of your body in these ways, you may find that you have more energy, feel more alert and focused, and are better able to manage stress.

Mental and emotional health are also key components of self-care and wellness. This can involve things like setting aside time to relax and de-stress, practicing mindfulness or meditation, or seeking out therapy or counseling when you need it. Taking care of your mental and emotional health can help you feel more resilient, cope with difficult situations more effectively, and enjoy a greater sense of inner peace and contentment.

Another important aspect of self-care and wellness is setting boundaries and recognizing your own needs. This means taking time for yourself when you need it, saying no to commitments that don't align with your values or priorities, and seeking support from others when you need it. Prioritizing self-care and wellness in this way can help you feel more balanced and fulfilled, which can ultimately lead to a happier, healthier life.

CHAPTER FOUR
CREATIVITY AND RESOURCEFULNESS

Creativity and resourcefulness are two distinct yet connected generalities that are frequently associated with problem-solving and invention.
Creativity is the ability to induce new and original ideas, generalities, or solutions. It involves using one's imagination to come up with ideas that are not immediately obvious or readily available. Creative thinking often involves breaking away from conventional or established patterns of thinking to come up with unique perspectives and approaches.

Resourcefulness, on the other hand, is the ability to find ways to overcome obstacles or achieve goals using the resources that are available. Resourceful individuals are able to think on their feet and adapt to changing circumstances, often by using their creativity to find innovative solutions.

Creativity and resourcefulness are both important for problem-solving and innovation. Creativity allows individuals to generate new and innovative ideas, while resourcefulness enables individuals to make the most of the resources available to them in order to bring those ideas to life.

In many ways, creativity and resourcefulness are complementary skills. Resourcefulness can help individuals implement creative ideas by finding ways to make them work within the constraints of the resources available. Creativity, on the other hand, can help individuals come up with new and innovative ways to use the resources that are available to them.

Overall, creativity and resourcefulness are important skills to cultivate, both individually and within organizations, as they can help drive innovation and problem-solving in a variety of contexts.

USING CREATIVITY AND RESOURCEFULNESS TO SOLVE PROBLEMS

Creativity and resourcefulness are essential skills for problem-solving. Here are some steps you can take to use your creativity and resourcefulness to solve problems:

1. **Define the problem**: Start by easily defining the problem you are trying to solve. This will help you focus your creativity and resourcefulness in the right direction.
2. **Brainstorm solutions:** Once you have defined the problem, brainstorm as many solutions as you can think of. Don't worry about whether they are practical or feasible at this point. Just focus on generating ideas.
3. **Evaluate solutions:** After you have a list of potential solutions, evaluate each one based on its feasibility, effectiveness, and cost. This will help you narrow down your options and choose the best solution.
4. **Be resourceful**: Think outside the box and consider all available resources. Can you repurpose something or use materials in a new way? Can you leverage technology or collaborate with others to find a solution?

5. **Iterate and refine:** As you implement your solution, be open to feedback and continue to refine your approach. Don't be panic to pivot if something isn't working.

By combining creativity and resourcefulness, you can tackle even the most challenging problems and come up with innovative solutions.

ALTERNATIVE WAYS TO ACQUIRE GOODS AND SERVICES

These alternative ways to acquire goods and services can be a useful skill to have, particularly in situations where traditional methods of acquisition may not be feasible or accessible. Here are some possible ways to acquire goods and services:

Bartering: Bartering involves trading goods or services with others without the use of money. For example, if you have a skill such as web design, you could offer to design a website for a small business owner in exchange for some of their products or services.

1. **Online marketplaces:** Online marketplaces such as eBay, Amazon, and Craigslist can be great places to find used or discounted goods. You can also find local buy-and-sell groups on social media platforms like Facebook.
2. **Sharing economy platforms**: Sharing economy platforms such as Airbnb, Uber, and TaskRabbit allow individuals to share goods and services with others for a fee. For example, you could rent out a spare room on Airbnb or offer your services as a handyman on TaskRabbit.
3. **Swapping**: Swapping involves exchanging goods or services with others without the use of money. For example, you could organize a clothing swap with friends or exchange language lessons with someone who wants to learn your native language.

4. **Free-cycling**: Free-cycling involves giving away unwanted goods for free to others who may need them. You can find local free-cycling groups on social media or through online platforms such as Freecycle.org.
5. **DIY:** If you have the skills and tools, you can make or repair items yourself instead of buying them. For example, you could make your own furniture or repair your own appliances instead of buying new ones.

By using these alternative methods to acquire goods and services, you can save money, reduce waste, and build relationships with others in your community.

CHAPTER FIVE
COMMUNITY INVOLVEMENT

Getting involved in local community initiatives: This can be a great way to make a positive impact in your neighborhood and to connect with like-minded individuals. It can also be a rewarding and fulfilling experience, as it allows you to make a positive impact on your community while also connecting with other like-minded individuals. Here are some steps you can take to get started:

1. **Identify the issues you care about:** Think about the issues that are most important to you and that you would like to see addressed in your community. These could be anything from environmental sustainability to social justice to education.
2. **Research local organizations:** Look for organizations in your community that are working on the issues you care about. This could include nonprofits, community groups, and grassroots organizations. You can do

research online, ask for recommendations from friends or family, or check with local government offices.
3. **Attend community events:** Attend community events related to the issues you care about. This could include rallies, meetings, or fundraisers. This will give you an opportunity to meet people who are passionate about the same things you are.
4. **Volunteer:** Many organizations are always looking for volunteers to help with their work. You can volunteer your time and skills to support their efforts.
5. **Start your own initiative:** If you don't find an organization that aligns with your interests, consider starting your own initiative. This could be as simple as organizing a neighborhood cleanup or starting a community garden.
6. **Stay informed:** Keep up-to-date with local news and events related to the issues you care about. This will help

you stay informed and know when there are opportunities to get involved.

Remember, getting involved in community initiatives takes time and effort, but the impact you can have can be significant. By working with others in your community, you can create positive change and make your neighborhood a better place for everyone.

BUILDING A SENSE OF COMMUNITY AND BELONGING

Building a sense of community and belonging refers to creating an environment in which individuals feel connected to each other and to a common purpose or goal. This can occur in various settings, such as a workplace, a neighborhood, a school, or a religious organization.

When individuals feel like they are part of a community, they experience a sense of belonging and connection to others, which can lead to increased feelings of happiness, satisfaction, and support. This feeling of connectedness is important for both

Affluence without money

individual well-being and the health of the community as a whole.

Building a sense of community and belonging can involve a range of strategies, such as fostering communication and interaction between community members, promoting shared values and goals, creating opportunities for collaboration and teamwork, and supporting the development of positive relationships and social connections. Ultimately, the goal is to create a welcoming and inclusive environment where everyone feels valued and supported.

CONCLUSION

A RECAP OF THE BENEFITS OF AFFLUENCE WITHOUT FINANCES

Affluence without finances refers to the idea of experiencing abundance and richness in life beyond material possessions and financial wealth. Some of the benefits of affluence without money include:

- Greater appreciation for non-material things: When we focus on what truly matters in life, we begin to appreciate intangible things such as good health, relationships, personal growth, and experiences.
- Increased happiness: Research suggests that material possessions do not necessarily lead to greater happiness. In fact, individuals who focus on non-material aspects of life tend to report higher levels of happiness and life satisfaction.
- Reduced stress: When we let go of the constant desire for more money and possessions, we can reduce the stress and pressure associated with striving

for financial success. This can lead to greater peace of mind and a more relaxed lifestyle.
- Enhanced relationships: Focusing on the people and experiences that matter most can lead to deeper, more meaningful relationships with loved ones.
- More time for hobbies and passions: By prioritizing what is truly important, we can free up time to pursue hobbies, passions, and other activities that bring us joy and fulfillment.

In summary, affluence without **finances** can lead to greater appreciation for non-material things, increased happiness, reduced stress, enhanced relationships, and more time for hobbies and passions.

ENCOURAGEMENT TO PURSUE A MORE FULFILLING AND MEANINGFUL LIFE

Encouragement to pursue a more fulfilling and meaningful life refers to providing support, motivation, and inspiration to someone who is seeking to improve their quality of life and find greater meaning and purpose in their daily experiences.
This can involve a variety of different strategies, including providing words of encouragement, offering practical advice and guidance, sharing personal experiences and insights, and providing emotional support during times of challenge or uncertainty.

The goal of encouragement to pursue a more fulfilling and meaningful life is to help individuals develop a clearer understanding of their values, passions, and goals and to support them in taking steps towards creating a life that aligns with their unique desires and aspirations. This may involve making changes to their career, relationships, lifestyle, or personal habits, and may require them to overcome obstacles and challenges along the way.

Ultimately, the purpose of encouragement to pursue a more fulfilling and meaningful life is to empower individuals to take control of their lives and to pursue a path that brings them greater happiness, satisfaction, and purpose.

www.ingramcontent.com/pod-product-compliance
Lightning Source LLC
Chambersburg PA
CBHW070956220526
45471CB00007B/3057